When Best Friends Aren't Forever

# When Best Friends *Aren't Forever*

A Faith-Filled Four-Week Guide for Healing After a Friendship Breakup

KRISTEN REED

RESOURCE *Publications* • Eugene, Oregon

WHEN BEST FRIENDS AREN'T FOREVER
A Faith-Filled Four-Week Guide for Healing After a Friendship Breakup

Copyright © 2024 Kristen Reed. All rights reserved. Except for brief quotations in critical publications or reviews, no part of this book may be reproduced in any manner without prior written permission from the publisher. Write: Permissions, Wipf and Stock Publishers, 199 W. 8th Ave., Suite 3, Eugene, OR 97401.

Resource Publications
An Imprint of Wipf and Stock Publishers
199 W. 8th Ave., Suite 3
Eugene, OR 97401

www.wipfandstock.com

PAPERBACK ISBN: 979-8-3852-0772-5
HARDCOVER ISBN: 979-8-3852-0773-2
EBOOK ISBN: 979-8-3852-0774-9

VERSION NUMBER 03/12/24

Scripture quotations are from the ESV® Bible (The Holy Bible, English Standard Version®), © 2001 by Crossway, a publishing ministry of Good News Publishers. Used by permission. All rights reserved. The ESV text may not be quoted in any publication made available to the public by a Creative Commons license. The ESV may not be translated in whole or in part into any other language.

To all my friends, past and present, who have helped me become the woman I am today, and to my best friend and partner for life, Noah.

"Now Barnabas wanted to take with them John called Mark. But Paul thought best not to take with them one who had withdrawn from them in Pamphylia and had not gone with them to the work. And there arose a sharp disagreement, so that they separated from each other."

ACTS 15:37-39 (PARTIAL)

# Contents

*Introduction* | ix

Day 1: It's Okay to Feel Like Crap. | 1
Day 2: Your Breakup Recovery Team | 3
Day 3: #Facts | 5
Day 4: Choose the Vine, Not the Wine. | 7
Day 5: You Know What They Say About Assuming. | 9
Day 6: Weekly Heart Check | 11
Day 7: Self-Care As Soul Care | 13
Day 8: It's You. Hi. You're (At Least Part of) the Problem. | 15
Day 9: Fighting Gossip | 17
Day 10: Tell Me Why! | 19
Day 11: Calendar Clean-Up | 21
Day 12: External Influences | 23
Day 13: Weekly Heart Check | 25
Day 14: Self-Care As Soul-Care | 27
Day 15: Stop Scrolling! | 29
Day 16: Praying Through the Pain | 32

## CONTENTS

Day 17: Counting the Cost | 34
Day 18: Remember What Remains. | 36
Day 19: Consider the Whole Person. | 38
Day 20: Weekly Heart Check | 40
Day 21: Self-Care As Soul-Care | 42
Day 22: Flourishing From Afar | 44
Day 23: Warning Signs for Next Time | 46
Day 24: Forgiveness, Redefined | 48
Day 25: A Wild Ex-BFF Suddenly Appears! | 50
Day 26: The End . . . Or Is It? | 52
Day 27: Weekly Heart Check | 55
Day 28: Self-Care As Soul-Care | 57

Final Thoughts | 59

*About the Author* | 61

# Introduction

Best friends.

Whether you're seven or thirty-seven, those two words can inspire a variety of memories and emotions.

- Wearing matching bracelets that fit together just as perfectly as you do
- Geeking out over your favorite bands at concerts
- Helping her find the wedding dress of her dreams
- Fuming over a passive-aggressive post she made on Instagram
- Grudgingly retiring an inside joke that only she would understand
- Blocking her on every social media platform you can think of
- Throwing that old bracelet in the garbage because you loathe her with the fire of a thousand suns, but you also miss her at the same time

Yeah . . . Many of us probably don't imagine the four unhappy occasions at the end of that list when we think about our

INTRODUCTION

best friends. But sometimes, the friendships we hope will last so long that we're picking out college majors, raising kids, and even retiring together end so abruptly that we're left with emotional whiplash. Experiencing the death of that crucial relationship can feel just as bad as (if not worse than) a breakup because you're used to the ups and downs of romance, but you never expected to watch your friendship crash and burn with an emotional journey that's worthy of a Taylor Swift breakup anthem.

I've gone through far more friendship breakups than I'd like to admit. And I don't just mean gradually drifting apart until you realize you haven't said a word to each other or hung out in years. I mean definitive breaks in friendships that involved betrayals, arguments, ugly emails, ugly crying, passive-aggressive Tweets, self-doubt, and lingering bitterness that took (and still takes) prayer, therapy, and self-discipline to tame.

I wish I could rewrite all those stories and save myself and my former friends a lot of drama, but God has used each conflict and the required healing to help me formulate some thoughts and practices I hope can help you start your journey to healing. And that's just what this is: a journey. Just as it can take months or years to go from strangers to best friends, it also takes time to start healing, fight bitterness, grow spiritually, and find peace after losing a friendship. I hope this book can help you do just that so you can move forward with a healthy perspective of the relationship you lost without being held back by blindness to your flaws or being hyper-focused on your friend's shortcomings.

This four-week workbook features five days of reading and processing each week, one weekly heart-check moment to help you monitor how you're processing your lost friendship emotionally, and one weekly Sabbath-inspired self-care activity. There will also be Scripture and prayer prompts throughout to help you keep God at the center of your healing process and keep your heart from becoming hard as you grieve and pray about the friendship you lost. So, grab a journal, pen, and a comforting cup of tea, and join me on the first leg of this journey from pain to peace.

## Day 1

# It's Okay to Feel Like Crap.

> "For it is not an enemy who taunts me—then I could bear it; it is not an adversary who deals insolently with me—then I could hide from him. But it is you, a man, my equal, my companion, my familiar friend."
>
> PSALM 55:12–13

MOST OF US WILL never experience the betrayal and peril that King David did in his many dramatic years on earth. But if you're reading this book, I bet his words from Psalm 55 made you feel a little knotted up inside. And that's okay! Having emotions is part of being human, and having strong, negative emotions is a natural part of the grieving process, whether you're mourning a death, breakup, or friendship. Even Jesus felt "sorrowful and troubled" as he prayed in Gethsemane before his arrest, and he *is* God, which means he knew his fate long before that morose moment in the garden and still had strong feelings about it.

So go ahead! Scream into a pillow if you're angry or weep if you're sad, but don't stop at just naming and feeling your emotions. Also, don't let your emotions guide how you treat others and process your lost friendship (Ephesians 4:26–27) because as real as your feelings are, they are not God's perfect truth. Part of growing in maturity and grieving well is using your emotions to assess your spiritual health just as you use a thermometer to assess your physical health. To get a little medical for a moment, if you take your temperature and realize that you have a fever, that elevated temperature is a sign that something is off, and you need a plan for healing. You may even need to bring other people into the situation so they can help as needed, depending on how severe the underlying infection is.

Similarly, when you realize you're having those understandably negative emotions about your former friend (or even yourself), bring God into those moments as King David often did in his psalms. Be brutally honest about how you *really* feel because he can take it, and ask him to help you find healing without sinning and making those emotions your master. God is intimately acquainted with how many tears you've cried (Psalm 56:8) and will wipe them all away when you're with him in eternity (Revelation 21:4), but he can start bringing you the guidance and comfort that you need right here, right now.

## APPLICATION

Write down the emotions you're struggling with, as well as the thoughts or events that are inspiring them, and ask God to help you process those emotions in a way that isn't harmful. If you have trouble identifying your emotions, search for a biblical emotions wheel online and use one as a resource. Share those feelings with a mature friend you trust to give wise counsel and admonish you if needed instead of just validating your emotions or pointing the blame at your former friend.

## Day 2

# Your Breakup Recovery Team

> "Oil and perfume make the heart glad, and the sweetness of a friend comes from his earnest counsel. [ . . . ] Iron sharpens iron, and one man sharpens another."
>
> PROVERBS 27:9, 17

ICE CREAM, CHICK FLICKS, and sassy affirmations with your friends all sound pretty nice when you're healing after a big breakup, whether romantic or platonic. But those coping mechanisms lack the depth needed to help us move forward as healed, hope-filled people. Proverbs 27 reminds us that people who give earnest counsel and sharpen us can positively affect our lives.

Sharpening can make sparks fly in a pretty unpleasant way, but it helps us become more spiritually mature and fruitful as believers than when people simply agree with us and bash the people we're in conflict with. When that truth-based counsel and admonishment are delivered with love, respect, and compassion, they can penetrate our hearts and help us respond to our BFF breakups in ways that lead to personal growth and healing without sinning against the people who hurt us. And pursuing a closer relationship with Jesus helps us find rest for our souls regardless of how we've been hurt or rejected (Matthew 11:28–30). By loving us with truth, our breakup recovery teams can help us love God *and* our former friends even from afar.

## APPLICATION

Spend some time identifying a few godly friends with whom you can process your former friendship. Think of people who regularly give biblical counsel and speak the truth in love, even in challenging situations. Then, ask God to help you pinpoint the best person to reach out to and give you wisdom about initiating a conversation with them.

# Day 3

# #Facts

> "A faithful witness does not lie, but
> a false witness breathes out lies."
>
> Proverbs 14:5

THE CONCEPT OF BEING a false witness often comes up in the Bible. From the Ten Commandments and proverbs to Jesus' and Stephen's trials before the Sanhedrin, we can see two things: God is not a fan of people who bear false witness and people who do so cause harm to others.

When a friendship ends, pain and pride can tempt you to skew your descriptions of how and why it ended so it sounds like you're 100 percent the hero (or victim) and your former BFF is 100 percent the enemy. That's why it's important to get an accurate view of the events that led up to your friendship ending. Whether you were 2 percent or 90 percent at fault, examining your actions so you can confess to God and make amends with whoever you hurt can help you glorify God while you grieve your broken friendship and process it with your breakup recovery team as needed. That honesty also enables you to love the friend you lost and makes it less messy to reconcile later if it's in the cards.

Also, I want to call out a key phrase I used in that last paragraph: "as needed." Not every conversation you or others might wish to have about your friendship breakup is necessary, loving, or constructive. Some people will cheer you on and disregard any wrong you did, some will pass along the juicy details you shared with others, and some are still friends with your ex-BFF and aren't mature enough to be there for you without feeling conflicted about what you share. So, as you work through your broken friendship, try to communicate what *really* happened with people who are mature and truly equipped to help you through it.

## APPLICATION

Write out the events and conversations that led to your friendship ending. Walk away from it for a few hours or days, then prayerfully reread what you wrote and see if you skewed anything in your favor or hers. Keep your findings in mind as you process your friendship breakup with others so you can talk about it constructively and with as little bias as possible.

*Day 4*

# Choose the Vine, Not the Wine.

> "And do not get drunk with wine, for that is debauchery, but be filled with the Spirit,"
>
> EPHESIANS 5:18

> "'I am the true vine, and my Father is the vinedresser.' [ . . . ] 'I am the vine; you are the branches. Whoever abides in me and I in him, he it is that bears much fruit, for apart from me you can do nothing.'"
>
> JOHN 15:1, 5

"I'M JUST A GIRL standing in front of grape juice, wishing it was merlot." If you've been on social media or in any home decor store in recent months, you've probably seen many memes, reels, to-go tumblers, and rustic wooden signs emblazoned with sassy statements like that about wine. I love a good merlot as much as the next girl, and I'm fairly certain that God is okay with wine since Jesus himself turned water into *good* wine at a wedding (John 2). Unfortunately, our culture has gotten to a place where it encourages us to seek solace from our work, motherhood, and relational woes with a long-stemmed glass or a freshly uncorked bottle filled with a certain buzz-inducing drink.

While alcohol in moderation and with the proper heart posture is not something to condemn, using it or other poor coping mechanisms to escape from our problems or numb our feelings doesn't truly help us process the pain we're struggling with. It only delays the inevitable processing and grieving we need to do to deal with our BFF breakups healthily, and it can inspire cringeworthy actions that can further rob us of health and peace.

So, if you're tempted to reach for the rosé (or cookies or joint or remote control) to deal with your former friendship, it's time to reach for the true vine and get a drink of living water from our Savior instead. Jesus will truly comfort you, heal the wounds that are causing so much pain right now, and help you grow spiritually because of your suffering so that one day, you can see the purpose behind your pain and comfort others (Romans 5:3–5 and 2 Corinthians 1:3–4). his love is better than any buzz.

## APPLICATION

List the coping mechanisms you've been using since your friendship began its decline—good and bad. This should include everything from binge-watching your favorite show to reading the Bible. Then, turn to God in prayer, and ask him to reveal which habits are helping your healing and which are hindering it.

## Day 5

# You Know What They Say About Assuming.

> "If one gives an answer before he hears,
> it is his folly and shame."
>
> PROVERBS 18:13

WE ALL LIKE TO make assumptions. As much as we wish we did, we don't have God's omniscience, and we like things to make sense sooner than they usually do, so we draw conclusions about people's words and actions based on the incomplete evidence (or intense feelings) we have at our disposal. Some assumptions are more accurate than others, but in the wake of a BFF breakup, they can often be overly charitable or overly condemning, depending on your disposition and where you are in the grieving process.

As I said, we all do this, but it's extremely helpful to be aware of your tendency to make assumptions and take those thoughts captive (2 Corinthians 10:4–5). That means combatting your negative assumptions with the truth about topics like humility, peacemaking, wisdom, and forgiveness to keep them from settling in and making a home in your heart.

## APPLICATION

What are some assumptions you've made about your ex-BFF? Are you assigning unspoken motives to her previous actions? Are you assuming that she's living her best life without you? Whatever those assumptions are, write them down, and ask God to clarify what is or was really going on and help you give less weight (if any) to your assumptions.

# Day 6

# Weekly Heart Check

ONE CONCEPT THAT I'VE heard many times over the years is that our feelings are real, but we shouldn't treat them like the truth. However, it is essential to name and acknowledge our feelings so we can bring them to God for comfort, counsel, and correction. With that in mind, take a few minutes to assess how you're feeling about your friendship breakup. Underline every emotion you're feeling, and circle the strongest three you're experiencing.

| Sad | Weary | Lonely | Hopeful | Peaceful |
|---|---|---|---|---|
| Anxious | Stressed out | Regretful | Accepting | Happy |
| Frustrated | Angry | Numb | Calm | Loved |
| Ashamed | Beaten down | Envious | Okay | Confident |
| Uncertain | Hopeless | Depressed | Positive | Relieved |

### REFLECTION

Take a moment to think and pray about what inspired the emotions you circled. Then, write down where those feelings are coming from and if you need counsel, comfort, and/or correction. For example, "I feel lonely because my ex-BFF was my roommate, and now I live alone. I might need counsel to figure out how to deal with my loneliness and whether I should get a new roommate." Lastly, share these findings with someone from your breakup recovery team so they can give you a biblical perspective about your feelings.

*Day 7*

# Self-Care As Soul Care

"Remember the sabbath day, to keep it holy. Six days you shall labor and do all your work, but the seventh day is a sabbath of the Lord your God; in it you shall not do any work, you or your son or your daughter, your male or your female servant or your cattle or your sojourner who stays with you. For in six days the Lord made the heavens and the earth, the sea and all that is in them, and rested on the seventh day; therefore the Lord blessed the sabbath day and made it holy."

Exodus 20:8–11

I RECENTLY NOTICED THAT in the English Standard Version of the Bible, the commandment about the Sabbath/rest is the longest of the Ten Commandments. It's really interesting to me that God spent more time explaining when, how, and why his people should rest than he did talking about idolatry, murder, etc. But when I think about how popular the "hustle hard" mindset is in our culture and the church, I can see why God elaborated on this commandment and even set the original example for rest when he created for six days and rested on the seventh.

Between work, hobbies, friendships, romantic relationships, kids, chores, girls' nights, side hustles, ministry, doom scrolling, streaming, and more, we don't give our bodies, minds, and hearts many chances to be still and be filled (Psalm 23 and Matthew 11:28-30). And yet, some things we do to chill out (like binge-watching *The Office* or videos on TikTok) give us a reprieve from physical activity without giving us the spiritual enrichment we need. Take a little time today to do a refreshing screen-free activity like the examples below, and consider praying or listening to the Bible while you do it. You could even focus on some passages that can help you process your emotions. A few of my favorites are Psalm 13, Psalm 31:23-24, Psalm 34:4-8, Psalm 42:5-6, Isaiah 40:29-31, Romans 5:3-5, Philippians 4:6-8, and James 1:19-20. Feel free to do more than one activity or combine a couple (like having a nice cup of coffee while you listen to worship music) if that would be spiritually enriching for you.

| Going for a walk, jog, or run | Reading or listening to a Christian book | Knitting or crocheting |
| --- | --- | --- |
| Gardening | Writing poetry | Drawing or painting |
| Using an adult coloring book | Cooking | Having a cup of coffee or tea |
| Swimming | Weightlifting | Riding a bike |
| Hiking | Getting a massage | Stretching |
| Listening to music | Playing a musical instrument | Taking a bath |

## Day 8

# It's You. Hi. You're (At Least Part of) the Problem.

"If we say we have no sin, we deceive ourselves, and the truth is not in us. If we confess our sins, he is faithful and just to forgive us our sins and to cleanse us from all unrighteousness. If we say we have not sinned, we make him a liar, and his word is not in us."

1 JOHN 1:8–10

IDENTIFYING YOUR SINS AND making a plan for repentance isn't exactly a fun activity. While the topic of looking inwardly, dying to self, and repenting of sin has been the focus of many books like *The Mortification of Sin* by John Owen, most Christians don't relish in the idea of taking a magnifying glass to their actions—let alone their actual motives. Yet, that is what today's devotional is all about.

Whether you had a life-crushing sin struggle that widened the chasm between you and your ex-BFF, you were just a little too snippy too often, or you were intentionally slow to reach out during a difficult season, we all have sin in our hearts that affects our words and actions. Having the faith and courage to look inwardly so you can identify and turn away from the sins and destructive patterns that you brought into your friendship can be a surprisingly freeing step that helps you not just heal but also be a better friend to everyone in your life in the months and years to come. And knowing that Jesus died for those sins and that God loves you perfectly can help you process your shortcomings with courage instead of shame.

## APPLICATION

Ask God to help you identify moments or patterns of sin that harmed your former friendship and how you should right those wrongs with your ex-BFF. That could look like reaching out to apologize now or planning to do so later. Even if she's not mature or healed enough to hear you out or respond well, remember that you're being faithful and glorifying God by making amends regardless of how she reacts. Then, reach out to your breakup recovery team or mentor to get some godly counsel on how to turn away from those sins and turn to walk with God.

*Day 9*

# Fighting Gossip

> "The mouths of fools are their undoing, and their lips are a snare to their very lives. The words of a gossip are like choice morsels; they go down to the inmost parts."
>
> Proverbs 18:7–8

Gossip feels good. Venting to someone indiscriminately or disguising bad-mouthing as a prayer request can bring you a short-lived sense of relief or power because you're reclaiming the narrative of your friendship breakup. It can also feel good to whoever you gossip with because they may feel pride because you chose to open up to them about your delicate situation. But when we bring our unresolved pain to people who are looking for choice morsels instead of those who will give biblical counsel, we're just digging a ditch of disdain instead of pursuing help and healing.

I've heard several pastors advise against bringing people into a situation if they aren't part of the problem or the solution, and I think that's a wise way to discern who you should process your BFF breakup with. When you're trying to decide which of your friends you should seek counsel from, ask yourself these questions:

- What am I trying to accomplish by sharing my story with them? Am I looking for validation and power or help and wisdom?

- Is this person spiritually mature enough to call out my sin and give me advice that will demonstrate love for my former friend and me?

- Am I willing to listen and change my behavior if they challenge my perspective or question my actions?

- Will this person honor my former friendship by not sharing the details about our friendship breakup with others unless it's truly helpful and necessary?

Of course, these questions aren't the only way to evaluate whether you're gossiping during a conversation about your former friendship, but they can help you identify some red flags so you can think twice before opening up. By exercising discernment in this area, you can love your former friend from afar and have a clean conscience about how you processed your friendship breakup.

## APPLICATION

Use the questions above to evaluate the nature of some of your recent conversations about your BFF breakup. If you notice a pattern of sharing details about your situation with the wrong motives or people, ask God to reveal how you can repent of that behavior and be wiser about seeking and applying wise counsel about your former friendship in the future.

## Day 10

# Tell Me Why!

"How long, O LORD? Will you forget me forever? How long will you hide your face from me? [...] But I have trusted in your steadfast love; my heart shall rejoice in your salvation. I will sing to the LORD, because he has dealt bountifully with me."

PSALM 13:1, 5–6

WHEN YOU'VE GONE THROUGH a challenging situation or season, the exclamation "Tell me why!" isn't just a lyric from an iconic Backstreet Boys song. It's one of the many questions you might be asking daily. Whether you're wondering why your friendship broke down, what signs you missed, or where you went wrong, I encourage you to take a page from King David's book. He started Psalm 13 by asking God questions about his situation in a way that revealed that his heart was in shambles at the moment. So, instead of swirling the toilet bowl of whys and what-ifs on his own, he asked the Creator of the universe about what was afflicting him.

But David didn't stop there.

Starting in verse five, the second King of Israel did what I like to call "turning the corner." He transitioned from asking questions and communicating his desperation to reaffirming his trust in and worship for God. This is *so* important! When we're in a difficult season, casting our anxieties on and posing our questions to God is crucial for our healing journey. But we also need to remind ourselves of who God is and how he has blessed and healed us in the past so that we don't lose sight of God's goodness and perfect love for us. And living by faith in this way helps us be conduits of God's goodness and love even when life feels bleak. That's why this psalm and many others are great models for how we can authentically process our questions and emotions but still be reverent and hopeful whether God answers our questions or not.

## APPLICATION

Write down some of your top questions about the end of your friendship. Then, write down three ways God has helped or blessed you recently. Once you're done, spend some time in prayer, asking God to reveal the answers you seek and thanking him for his love and kindness.

*Day 11*

# Calendar Clean-Up

"Commit your work to the Lord, and your plans will be established."

Proverbs 16:3

When you care about someone, you often make long-term plans. That could be anything from renewing a lease if you're roommates to buying tickets for a concert you've been *dying* to check out together. So, when a friendship ends, you might wind up with some unwanted reminders or events you need to strategize about on your calendar. Even memories on Facebook can be a minefield when a trip down yesteryear inspires tears and rage instead of wistful nostalgia.

These awkward, punched-in-the-stomach feelings can sometimes be avoidable, which is why being proactive and surrendering these events to God is so important. Identifying triggers, potential cancellations, and plan shifts can help you face each day (and each potential run-in) with love, kindness, and prayerful preparation instead of the anxiety and defensiveness that can spike when you feel blindsided. So be prayerful with your planning as you navigate these first months after your BFF breakup.

## APPLICATION

Look ahead at your calendar and make a list of events you planned to attend with your ex-BFF as well as ones where you might run into her. Also, include holidays and other significant dates like birthdays that might be difficult. Then, prayerfully formulate a plan for how you should approach each one, whether that means canceling your plans or spiritually preparing for how you can honor God in your interactions if you run into your ex-BFF. If you do or planned to live together, create a plan for finding a new place to live, whether that means living with your family, roommates, or alone.

## Day 12

# External Influences

"Once when Jacob was cooking stew, Esau came in from the field, and he was exhausted. And Esau said to Jacob, 'Let me eat some of that red stew, for I am exhausted!' (Therefore his name was called Edom.) Jacob said, 'Sell me your birthright now.' Esau said, 'I am about to die; of what use is a birthright to me?' Jacob said, 'Swear to me now.' So he swore to him and sold his birthright to Jacob. Then Jacob gave Esau bread and lentil stew, and he ate and drank and rose and went his way. Thus Esau despised his birthright."

GENESIS 25:29–34

IN A WORLD FULL of social media algorithms, elections, stressful jobs, complicated family dynamics, social justice movements, and global pandemics, we have a lot of external factors that can affect our relationships for the good, the bad, or both.

I chose the above verses from Genesis because they're a great depiction of how an external factor like hunger can affect someone's behavior. Esau did something he regretted because of his hunger, and it soured his already strained relationship with his twin brother. For me, I've dealt with BFF breakups in the wake of my mom dying of cancer, during the coronavirus pandemic, and more. While there were a lot of conflicts, conversations, and unresolved issues at play in those circumstances, it's clear in retrospect that those life- and world-changing events negatively affected those relationships because they first affected my or their spiritual and mental health. Now the question is, what external factors were at play in your situation?

## APPLICATION

Take a few moments to think through anything significant—good or bad—outside of your friendship that may have affected how y'all treated each other or responded to conflict. This could be everything from death and marriage to career changes and moving. Then, write down how they may have strained y'all's patience, kindness, emotional resilience, energy levels, etc. during the months leading up to your breakup.

*Day 13*

# Weekly Heart Check

OUR FEELINGS ARE REAL, but we shouldn't treat them like the truth. However, it is essential to name and acknowledge our feelings so we can bring them to God for comfort, counsel, and correction. With that in mind, take a few minutes to assess how you're feeling about your friendship breakup. Underline every emotion you're feeling, and circle the strongest three you're experiencing.

| Sad | Weary | Lonely | Hopeful | Peaceful |
|---|---|---|---|---|
| Anxious | Stressed out | Regretful | Accepting | Happy |
| Frustrated | Angry | Numb | Calm | Loved |
| Ashamed | Beaten down | Envious | Okay | Confident |
| Uncertain | Hopeless | Depressed | Positive | Relieved |

### REFLECTION

Take a moment to think and pray about what inspired the emotions you circled. Then, write down where those feelings are coming from and if you need counsel, comfort, and/or correction. For example, "I feel lonely because my ex-BFF was my roommate, and now I live alone. I might need counsel to figure out

how to deal with my loneliness and whether I should get a new roommate." Lastly, share these findings with someone from your breakup recovery team so they can give you a biblical perspective about your feelings.

*Day 14*

# Self-Care As Soul-Care

"Remember the sabbath day, to keep it holy. Six days you shall labor and do all your work, but the seventh day is a sabbath of the Lord your God; in it you shall not do any work, you or your son or your daughter, your male or your female servant or your cattle or your sojourner who stays with you. For in six days the Lord made the heavens and the earth, the sea and all that is in them, and rested on the seventh day; therefore the Lord blessed the sabbath day and made it holy."

Exodus 20:8–11

In the English Standard Version of the Bible, the commandment about the Sabbath/rest is the longest of the Ten Commandments. It's really interesting to me that God spent more time explaining when, how, and why his people should rest than he did talking about idolatry, murder, etc. But when I think about how popular the "hustle hard" mindset is in our culture and the church, I can see why God elaborated on this commandment and even set the original example for rest when he created for six days and rested on the seventh.

## WHEN BEST FRIENDS AREN'T FOREVER

Between work, hobbies, friendships, romantic relationships, kids, chores, girls' nights, side hustles, ministry, doom scrolling, streaming, and more, we don't give our bodies, minds, and hearts many chances to be still and be filled (Psalm 23 and Matthew 11:28–30). And yet, some things we do to chill out (like binge-watching *The Office* or videos on TikTok) give us a reprieve from physical activity without giving us the spiritual enrichment we need. Take a little time today to do a refreshing screen-free activity like the examples below, and consider praying or listening to the Bible while you do it. You could even focus on some passages that can help you process your emotions. A few of my favorites are Psalm 13, Psalm 31:23–24, Psalm 34:4–8, Psalm 42:5–6, Isaiah 40:29–31, Romans 5:3–5, Philippians 4:6–8, and James 1:19–20. Feel free to do more than one activity or combine a couple (like having a nice cup of coffee while you listen to worship music) if that would be spiritually enriching for you.

| | | |
|---|---|---|
| Going for a walk, jog, or run | Reading or listening to a Christian book | Knitting or crocheting |
| Gardening | Writing poetry | Drawing or painting |
| Using an adult coloring book | Cooking | Having a cup of coffee or tea |
| Swimming | Weightlifting | Riding a bike |
| Hiking | Getting a massage | Stretching |
| Listening to music | Playing a musical instrument | Taking a bath |

*Day 15*

# Stop Scrolling!

"Finally, brothers, whatever is true, whatever is honorable, whatever is just, whatever is pure, whatever is lovely, whatever is commendable, if there is any excellence, if there is anything worthy of praise, think about these things."

Philippians 4:8

When you think of the content you consume on Instagram, TikTok, or your favorite social media app, what comes to mind? My feeds are a mix of parenting advice, cat memes, devotional-style content, crunchy lifestyle tips, goofy videos, memories, and updates from my favorite friends, brands, and ministries. Seeing what's new on social media is usually interesting, if not fun, but those scrolling sessions can be like walking through an emotional minefield during those first weeks or months after a friendship breakup. You might see a meme that you immediately want to share with your former friend, old posts about moments y'all shared, or other people tagging her in posts. Those unwanted reminders paired with ill-timed posts about friendship or conflict that the algorithm thinks you might like can be a recipe for bitterness, anger, and sadness. And creeping on your former friend's profiles usually isn't any better for your heart. Those emotionally charged social moments are why adjusting your preferences on social media can be helpful for your healing journey.

Another thing to consider is priming your heart with the truth before that first-thing-in-the-morning or last-thing-before-bedtime doom scroll. Philippians 4:8 lists several adjectives describing what we should fill our thoughts with, and God is the epitome of all those things. He is true, pure, honorable, just, and so much more, which is why we need to fill our hearts with his Word before we open them up to the world's influence. Our only weapon in the armor of God is the "sword of the Spirit, which is the word of God" (Ephesians 6:17, partial), and the last thing we should do when fighting for our hearts and minds during a difficult season is go to war unarmed.

## APPLICATION

First, I'll address the algorithm issue. When content comes up that hinders your spiritual recovery from your BFF breakup, consider hiding the post or unfollowing the account that posted it. This means anything that makes you feel justified in hating or not forgiving your ex-BFF. Content that merely inspires sadness because it reminds you about your loss might not be worth kicking to the curb, but things that inspire and encourage an un-Christian attitude of unforgiveness and bitterness are worth a good "hide" or "unfollow." This removes the post in question and can discourage the platform from suggesting similar content in the future.

It can also be helpful to temporarily block your former friend. Your primary motivation for doing this should be to remove the temptation to creep on her posts if doing so makes you spiral into unhealthy, hateful thoughts, *not to circumvent forgiveness and reconciliation.* I recommend processing this decision with someone from your BFF breakup recovery team so you can ensure you're doing so for the right reasons and determine if you need to proactively communicate your intentions to your ex-BFF to prevent further hurt or misunderstandings.

## STOP SCROLLING!

Also, set an alarm on your phone to start and/or end your day in the Bible. If you don't know what to read during that planned time, try downloading an app with free or affordable Bible study plans or devotionals. You could also just pick a book of the Bible to focus on and keep your Bible on your bedside table so you can reach it just as easily as your phone.

## Day 16

# Praying Through the Pain

"After the LORD had spoken these words to Job, the LORD said to Eliphaz the Temanite: 'My anger burns against you and against your two friends, for you have not spoken of me what is right, as my servant Job has. Now therefore take seven bulls and seven rams and go to my servant Job and offer up a burnt offering for yourselves. And my servant Job shall pray for you, for I will accept his prayer not to deal with you according to your folly. For you have not spoken of me what is right, as my servant Job has.'"

JOB 42:7–8

JOB HAD IT ROUGH. Even though he was "a blameless and upright man" (Job 1:8) by God's standards, he still lost his children, servants, livestock, and health in what probably felt like the blink of an eye. As if that wasn't bad enough, the people left in his life weren't exactly encouraging. His wife told him to "Curse God and die," and his friends accused him of having some sort of hidden sin that caused his many calamities. Job and his questionable friends went back and forth for nearly forty chapters, debating their conclusions and accusations about his plight until God finally stepped in. Part of God's intervention included a call for Job to pray for the very people who added insult to injury during what was likely the most challenging season of his life.

Job's obedient prayer for his friends and passages like Luke 6:27–31 are great reminders to pray not just for our hearts and circumstances but for the very people who hurt us, whether they are friends, former friends, or enemies. And I don't just mean prayers that give imprecatory psalm vibes. I mean praying for their healing and spiritual growth because their hurtful actions that led to the schism in your relationship could indicate a great spiritual struggle or a deep hurt that may be completely separate from your conflict. Your ex-BFF needs comfort, love, and redirection, just like you do, so praying for her is an amazing way to love her from afar and fight the bitterness that is crouching at the door of your heart.

## APPLICATION

Take five minutes today to pray for your former friend. If you're drawing a blank about what to pray, you can start by praying for her spiritual and mental health and for her to have clarity and conviction about what happened in your friendship as well as how to respond to it. If you feel led, you can also set an alarm to pray for your old friend weekly so you can regularly exercise your prayer muscle and wage war on the temptation to vilify your ex-BFF instead of forgiving her as God calls you to.

# Day 17

# Counting the Cost

> "Then Job arose and tore his robe and shaved his head and fell on the ground and worshiped. And he said, 'Naked I came from my mother's womb, and naked shall I return. The LORD gave, and the LORD has taken away; blessed be the name of the LORD.' In all this Job did not sin or charge God with wrong."
>
> JOB 1:20–22

SOME PEOPLE MIGHT SAY that mourning and lamenting are lost arts in our modern culture. We can be so focused on putting on a brave face, exuding sass, or hiding our pain that we try to sweep our grief aside instead of truly processing it and bringing it to God. Yet the Bible depicts Job and others mourning, has a whole book called Lamentations (which has acrostic poetry mourning Jerusalem's destruction), and features over fifty individual and communal psalms of lament. So, mourning *clearly* matters. But to mourn something thoroughly, you must identify what you lost.

In your case, you lost a friend, but what little things did you lose because your friendship crumbled? With some of my previous friendship breakdowns, I lost concert buddies, people to share inside jokes with, a go-to girlfriend to share good and bad news with, and so much more. I bet you'd have a similar list of losses if you sat down and processed the domino effect of your friendship breakup. While it's not fun to dig deep and identify those losses, God is faithful to comfort us during hard times (Matthew 5:4 and 2 Corinthians 1:3–4), and intentionally itemizing those losses now can help you be more prepared when you encounter reminders about them in the future. With that in mind, it's time to name the burdens and anxieties left by your BFF breakup and cast them on the Lord so he can sustain you with his perfect love (1 Peter 5:7).

## APPLICATION

Spend some time today listing the specific things you lost because your friendship ended. These could be physical losses like a ride to work, emotional losses like having someone to confide in, or even financial ones like spending more money on rent or bills because you lost a roommate. Then, share these losses with God in prayer, asking him to heal your hurts, meet your needs, and give you the wisdom you need to respond to these losses in a godly way.

## Day 18

# Remember What Remains.

> "Rejoice always, pray without ceasing, give thanks in all circumstances; for this is the will of God in Christ Jesus for you."
>
> 1 THESSALONIANS 5:16–18

PAUL'S COMMANDS ABOUT REJOICING and giving thanks might make some of us scratch our heads and squint a bit as we question the strength of his words. We incredulously ponder his use of the word *"always"* and the phrase *"in all circumstances,"* questioning the wisdom behind such inescapable demands. But when we think about Paul's life and what he might fold into his "always" and "all circumstances," a little humility might set in. He was imprisoned, beaten, shipwrecked, in danger many times, sleep deprived, and so much more (2 Corinthians 11:16–28). This is the same man who was literally singing hymns to God in prison while he was restrained in stocks (Acts 16:23–28).

Before we go any further, I must emphasize that I'm not describing Paul's plights to minimize yours.

Pain is pain, and it requires comfort and compassion, whether that pain stems from a difficult day at work, a broken friendship, or an unjust prison sentence. Instead, I shared Paul's story to show you that it *is* possible to be grateful and find joy even on your darkest days because God is with you—loving you even at your worst (Romans 5:8) and sanctifying you perfectly (Philippians 1:6). And since every good and perfect gift comes from him (James 1:17), you can give God credit and thank him for every remaining friend, paycheck, hot meal, and beautiful sunset you get to experience, even after losing a close friendship. Does this mean you should slap on a fake smile or stuff how the tough stuff makes you feel? By no means! I'm simply encouraging you to recognize the good you still have during a bad season and express gratitude to God for his never-ending faithfulness even as you tearfully entreat him for comfort and strength.

## APPLICATION

Write down five things in your life that you're thankful for. Then, spend a little time thanking God for those things through prayer. If any items on your gratitude list are people, consider shooting them a text or calling them to share how you're grateful for them. You might just make their day!

*Day 19*

# Consider the Whole Person.

> "I will remember the deeds of the LORD; yes, I will remember your wonders of old. I will ponder all your work, and meditate on your mighty deeds. Your way, O God, is holy. What god is great like our God?"
>
> PSALM 77:11–13

WHEN ANY KIND OF relationship ends, whether romantic or platonic, it can be tempting to hyperfocus on the bad that happened and the many ways we were wronged. And while this internal character assassination might make us feel vindicated or unjustly victimized, it doesn't do justice to the relationship that has us all riled up. Instead, we need to zoom out and see our former friend as a whole person who has vices, victories, virtues, and more. We also need to acknowledge the good they did in our lives and the joy they inspired instead of only focusing on the pain and disillusionment they caused.

King David did this briefly in Psalm 55, which *really* hits differently after a BFF breakup. In verse 14, he says, "We used to take sweet counsel together; within God's house we walked in the throng." It's a bittersweet moment of reflection in a psalm that's full of anguish, indignation, prayer, and even some imprecatory

CONSIDER THE WHOLE PERSON.

vibes about a profound betrayal he endured. As we discussed yesterday, every good thing comes from God, so when we acknowledge our old friend's good qualities and the fun memories we shared, we're not just remembering the good old days. We're also calling to mind how God has shown us his goodness through our old friend... even if those glimmers of his goodness and glory seem a lifetime away.

## APPLICATION

Grab your journal and allow yourself to zoom out from the plight and pain your BFF breakup caused so that you can remember the good about your friendship. Start by writing out Genesis 1:26–27 and Psalm 139:23–24 to remind yourself that God made your ex-BFF in his image. Write down some of the quirks and qualities that you loved about your friend, and even note a few of your favorite memories together. You may need to refer to this when you feel tempted to vilify your former friend and see her negatively or one-dimensionally. Then, pray to God and thank him for the kindness and love he showed you through your old friend.

## Day 20

# Weekly Heart Check

OUR FEELINGS ARE REAL, but we shouldn't treat them like the truth. However, it is essential to name and acknowledge our feelings so we can bring them to God for comfort, counsel, and correction. With that in mind, take a few minutes to assess how you're feeling about your friendship breakup. Underline every emotion you're feeling, and circle the strongest three you're experiencing.

| Sad | Weary | Lonely | Hopeful | Peaceful |
| --- | --- | --- | --- | --- |
| Anxious | Stressed out | Regretful | Accepting | Happy |
| Frustrated | Angry | Numb | Calm | Loved |
| Ashamed | Beaten down | Envious | Okay | Confident |
| Uncertain | Hopeless | Depressed | Positive | Relieved |

**REFLECTION**

Take a moment to think and pray about what inspired the emotions you circled. Then, write down where those feelings are coming from and if you need counsel, comfort, and/or correction. For example, "I feel lonely because my ex-BFF was my roommate, and now I live alone. I might need counsel to figure out

how to deal with my loneliness and whether I should get a new roommate." Lastly, share these findings with someone from your breakup recovery team so they can give you a biblical perspective about your feelings.

## Day 21

# Self-Care As Soul-Care

"Remember the sabbath day, to keep it holy. Six days you shall labor and do all your work, but the seventh day is a sabbath of the Lord your God; in it you shall not do any work, you or your son or your daughter, your male or your female servant or your cattle or your sojourner who stays with you. For in six days the Lord made the heavens and the earth, the sea and all that is in them, and rested on the seventh day; therefore the Lord blessed the sabbath day and made it holy."

Exodus 20:8–11

In the English Standard Version of the Bible, the commandment about the Sabbath/rest is the longest of the Ten Commandments. It's really interesting to me that God spent more time explaining when, how, and why his people should rest than he did talking about idolatry, murder, etc. But when I think about how popular the "hustle hard" mindset is in our culture and the church, I can see why God elaborated on this commandment and even set the original example for rest when he created for six days and rested on the seventh.

## SELF-CARE AS SOUL-CARE

Between work, hobbies, friendships, romantic relationships, kids, chores, girls' nights, side hustles, ministry, doom scrolling, streaming, and more, we don't give our bodies, minds, and hearts many chances to be still and be filled (Psalm 23 and Matthew 11:28–30). And yet, some things we do to chill out (like binge-watching *The Office* or videos on TikTok) give us a reprieve from physical activity without giving us the spiritual enrichment we need. Take a little time today to do a refreshing screen-free activity like the examples below, and consider praying or listening to the Bible while you do it. You could even focus on some passages that can help you process your emotions. A few of my favorites are Psalm 13, Psalm 31:23–24, Psalm 34:4–8, Psalm 42:5–6, Isaiah 40:29–31, Romans 5:3–5, Philippians 4:6–8, and James 1:19–20. Feel free to do more than one activity or combine a couple (like having a nice cup of coffee while you listen to worship music) if that would be spiritually enriching for you.

| | | |
|---|---|---|
| Going for a walk, jog, or run | Reading or listening to a Christian book | Knitting or crocheting |
| Gardening | Writing poetry | Drawing or painting |
| Using an adult coloring book | Cooking | Having a cup of coffee or tea |
| Swimming | Weightlifting | Riding a bike |
| Hiking | Getting a massage | Stretching |
| Listening to music | Playing a musical instrument | Taking a bath |

# Day 22

# Flourishing From Afar

"And after some days Paul said to Barnabas, 'Let us return and visit the brothers in every city where we proclaimed the word of the Lord, and see how they are.' Now Barnabas wanted to take with them John called Mark. But Paul thought best not to take with them one who had withdrawn from them in Pamphylia and had not gone with them to the work. And there arose a sharp disagreement, so that they separated from each other. Barnabas took Mark with him and sailed away to Cyprus, but Paul chose Silas and departed, having been commended by the brothers to the grace of the Lord. And he went through Syria and Cilicia, strengthening the churches."

ACTS 15:36–41

THIS PASSAGE FROM ACTS has been on my mind since I decided to write this book. I find it so interesting that this moment of relational strife between Paul and Barnabas didn't just happen. It was recorded in Scripture for us to read and analyze for thousands of years. Paul was gun-shy about John Mark because of some past disappointments, but Barnabas didn't share Paul's conviction about John Mark. So, they had a "sharp disagreement" and went their separate ways. We'll come back to this passage at the end of the book, but today, I want to focus on the fact that both men and their travel companions continued their ministry work even though they experienced intense conflict.

While you and your ex-BFF were probably not on the verge of embarking on an epic missionary journey together, God has marked out journeys for each of you that involve numerous opportunities to glorify and lean on him. If you're both followers of Christ, you have the Holy Spirit dwelling in you and enabling you to do good works in God's name, whether you resume your friendship tomorrow, in five years, or never. That means you can love your friend from afar by hoping that she flourishes in her faith regardless of the state of your friendship, and you can focus on doing the same yourself.

## APPLICATION

If your former friend is a Christian, ask God to help your friend be a faithful follower of Christ in whatever ways God calls her to. This could be through work, ministry, marriage, parenthood, hobbies, and more. Pray for God to help her thrive and glorify him in those areas despite whatever hurts she is dealing with in light of your BFF breakup. Then, pray for all those things for yourself as well. If your ex-BFF is not a Christian, pray for her to hear and believe the gospel so she can experience God's grace and purpose for her life just as you have.

## Day 23

# Warning Signs for Next Time

"The prudent sees danger and hides himself, but the simple go on and suffer for it."

Proverbs 22:3

Uncle Ben from the Spider-Man comic books is often quoted because he uttered these words before his untimely death, "With great power comes great responsibility." Today, I'd like to add that *knowledge* also comes with responsibility. In the case of your friendship ending, you've had about three weeks to process what happened through the tools and prompts provided in this book. As you think about what went wrong and what those mistakes (whether yours or hers) cost you, you might wish that you could change the past and interact with her based on this newfound knowledge. Unfortunately, that's not possible unless you live in the Marvel Cinematic Universe and have access to time machines and Infinity Stones like our favorite web-slinger and his buddies.

However, you *can* take what you've learned and apply that knowledge to your current and future friendships. If you realize that you need to follow up more when a friend is struggling, keep an eye out for opportunities to do that in the future. If codependency contributed to your friendship ending, be on the lookout for a rescuer-rescuee dynamic so you can address it before it goes too far. If you tend to avoid conflict until things are about to explode, pray through how to keep short accounts by addressing conflict with your loved ones promptly.

Whether reconciliation is in God's plans for your broken friendship or not, you can move forward and react to the warning signs and unhealthy patterns you've identified so you can proactively address conflict and pursue relational health instead of suffering more because you didn't apply what you learned. You can't control what other people do or prevent external factors like election results and pandemics, but you can love the people around you by prayerfully applying what you've learned during this process.

## APPLICATION

Flip through your journal entries from the past twenty-two days of devotionals, and list things that negatively impacted your friendship and could be potential pitfalls in your current and future relationships. Then, pray for God to open your heart and eyes so that you can perceive and proactively address unhealthy behaviors/patterns and external factors when they begin to influence your relationships.

## Day 24

# Forgiveness, Redefined

> "Put on then, as God's chosen ones, holy and beloved, compassionate hearts, kindness, humility, meekness, and patience, bearing with one another and, if one has a complaint against another, forgiving each other; as the Lord has forgiven you, so you also must forgive."
>
> COLOSSIANS 3:12–13

FORGIVENESS IS ONE OF the best things you can do after you've been hurt. It can also be one of the most difficult for two reasons: a lack of understanding about what forgiveness is and a lack of regret from the person who hurt you. People often use the phrase "forgive and forget," and because it seems impossible to forget the hurt we've sustained, forgiveness also seems impossible. But forgiveness is about *releasing*, not forgetting or condoning someone's sinful behavior. To forgive someone who wronged you is to trust God to deal with their sin with justice, mercy, or both and to fight bitterness whenever it rises within you.

Forgiveness is also separate from reconciliation. That means your ex-BFF doesn't need to express sorrow over what she did, change her ways, or become your friend again for you to forgive her. You can forgive her right here, right now, even if you haven't spoken in months and even if she's still pursuing the same self-destructive, relationship-harming behaviors that tore your friendship apart.

With that in mind, I love how today's passage from Colossians begins and ends. We start with the command to put on the virtues Paul lists and end with the command to forgive as God has forgiven us. The beginning is a reminder that this attitude doesn't come naturally to us. We must actively work to be compassionate, kind, humble, etc., by submitting to the Holy Spirit instead of our flesh. When it comes to God's much-needed forgiveness, I also like to think of Romans 5:8. Jesus died for us while we were still sinners, and our justification before God comes when we *believe*, not when we behave. God forgives us and sees us as righteous before he beautifully wrecks shop in our hearts to make us more like him. Since the call in Colossians 3:13 is to forgive as God forgives, that means that we can stop poisoning our hearts with enmity and bitterness toward our former friends before they change . . . and even if they never do.

## APPLICATION

As I said, forgiveness can be extremely hard, so your application for today isn't to forgive your former friend. Instead, use your journaling time to write down what (if anything) is keeping you from forgiving her. Then, ask God to help you overcome those obstacles so you can forgive her as he forgave you. Also, ask him to help your friend grow and heal so she can forgive you for any pain you caused her.

## Day 25

# A Wild Ex-BFF Suddenly Appears!

> "Repay no one evil for evil, but give thought to do what is honorable in the sight of all. If possible, so far as it depends on you, live peaceably with all. Beloved, never avenge yourselves, but leave it to the wrath of God, for it is written, 'Vengeance is mine, I will repay, says the Lord.'"
>
> ROMANS 12:17–19

ONE OF THE MOST stressful things about venturing into the world after a friendship breakup is wondering when you'll finally have that awkward moment of running into your former friend. If you're anything like me, your imagination runs wild in the worst way as you imagine what will happen when you finally face each other. Will she be nice? Will she start drama? Will *I* start drama? Will I say something weird or embarrassing? Will she act like I don't even exist?

Whether your potential run-in is a wedding, church service, or concert, something that would normally be a fun occasion is suddenly marked by anxiety (and maybe preemptive indignation) instead of joyful anticipation. Since we know these situations can be so stressful, taking the time to look ahead at your calendar and prepare your heart is so important. I addressed the calendar management aspect of this on day 11, so today I'm addressing the heart preparation.

I love this passage from Romans 12 because of one key phrase, "so far as it depends on you." This is important because God calls us to be peacemakers *regardless of other people's behavior*. So, if your ex-BFF is spiteful, respond with love and maturity instead of spite. If she acts awkwardly, respond with kindness instead of assuming negative intent or being smug because she embarrassed herself.

As this passage reminds us, God ultimately judges our hearts and behavior. When you have a right view of your flaws and shortcomings *and* in light of your friendship breakup, you know God's judgment also extends to you. Being aware of your sinful moments and patterns can be a necessary reminder that both of you need God's grace to save you from your sins and help you live rightly by his standards. Thanks to that self-awareness, you can respond to your former friend with love and humility, whether she acts like you don't exist, glares at you from across the room, or gives you a hug you didn't even realize you needed.

## APPLICATION

Refer to your list of upcoming events from day 11 or write down the upcoming events where you might run into your former BFF. Then, use your favorite calendar or reminder app to set reminders to pray for both of you to honor God and try to love one another during whatever interactions you have, regardless of the other person's behavior. I suggest reading Luke 6:27–31 as inspiration for loving your former friend even when she feels like an enemy.

## Day 26

# The End... Or Is It?

"Therefore, if anyone is in Christ, he is a new creation. The old has passed away; behold, the new has come. All this is from God, who through Christ reconciled us to himself and gave us the ministry of reconciliation;"

2 CORINTHIANS 5:17–18

GOD HAS GIVEN US a lot of amazing things, including the ministry of reconciliation, and the most important person to whom we can be reconciled is God. He forgives us for our sins when we believe that Jesus died for our sins (and rose from the dead as the ultimate sign that the payment cleared), and he entreats us to turn from our sins to walk with him. Because God paid the price to bring us into a right relationship with him, Christians should know how important and beautiful forgiveness and repentance are. That's why we should keep our hearts open to reconciling with our former friends. But what does that look like when you've been deeply hurt and don't see any signs of reconciliation?

Work on your own heart, and pray for hers.

Reconciliation requires two things that our flesh *loves* to fight against: mutual forgiveness and mutual repentance. As I said on day 24, forgiving someone means trusting God to deal with their sin with justice, mercy, or both, and committing to fighting bitterness. This ongoing discipline requires more work on some days than others, depending on what's going on in your mind, heart, and life. Repentance is a similarly ongoing practice that involves acknowledging your sins, turning away from those sins, and fleeing temptation so that you can live in a way that pleases God. Both forgiveness and repentance must be present for you to have true reconciliation, so if one of you isn't willing to do that hard spiritual work, you won't truly be reconciled even if you're mature enough to be kind to one another during the occasional run-in.

And reconciliation doesn't necessarily mean returning to being best friends as if nothing happened. You will likely need to start *slowly* with a more casual friendship and build up to greater emotional intimacy as you grow to trust each other more. So, resist the urge to go back to texting all the time, hanging out all weekend, etc. until you've both truly come to terms with your falling out and have a plan for how to have a healthy friendship going forward. It's also fine to stay at that more casual but reconciled level indefinitely because of how your lives have changed and how you've matured since your friendship ended. For example, if one of you moved farther away or went through a drastic life change that requires different priorities (like taking a more demanding job, getting married, or becoming a mom), you might not logistically be able to spend as much quality time together even if you have the best intentions. And that's perfectly okay!

Either way, you may need to start that renewed friendship with an honest conversation about what happened and how to have a healthy friendship with loving, open, mature communication going forward. But whatever happens, keep your heart open to reconciliation by exercising your forgiveness and repentance muscles and praying for your former friend to do the same.

## APPLICATION

What, if anything, is keeping you from being reconciled with your former friend? Spend some time journaling about your hesitations and whose forgiveness or repentance stands in your way. Then pray for God to give you guidance about how to handle that reconciliation gap. Also, commit to regularly (daily, weekly, monthly, or even annually on her birthday) praying that your former friend would do the work of repentance and forgiveness so that her heart is also primed for a potential reconciliation.

*Day 27*

# Weekly Heart Check

OUR FEELINGS ARE REAL, but we shouldn't treat them like the truth. However, it is essential to name and acknowledge our feelings so we can bring them to God for comfort, counsel, and correction. With that in mind, take a few minutes to assess how you're feeling about your friendship breakup. Underline every emotion you're feeling, and circle the strongest three you're experiencing.

| Sad | Weary | Lonely | Hopeful | Peaceful |
|---|---|---|---|---|
| Anxious | Stressed out | Regretful | Accepting | Happy |
| Frustrated | Angry | Numb | Calm | Loved |
| Ashamed | Beaten down | Envious | Okay | Confident |
| Uncertain | Hopeless | Depressed | Positive | Relieved |

**REFLECTION**

Take a moment to think and pray about what inspired the emotions you circled. Then, write down where those feelings are coming from and if you need counsel, comfort, and/or correction. For example, "I feel lonely because my ex-BFF was my roommate, and now I live alone. I might need counsel to figure out

how to deal with my loneliness and whether I should get a new roommate." Lastly, share these findings with someone from your breakup recovery team so they can give you a biblical perspective about your feelings.

# Day 28

# Self-Care As Soul-Care

> "Remember the sabbath day, to keep it holy. Six days you shall labor and do all your work, but the seventh day is a sabbath of the LORD your God; in it you shall not do any work, you or your son or your daughter, your male or your female servant or your cattle or your sojourner who stays with you. For in six days the LORD made the heavens and the earth, the sea and all that is in them, and rested on the seventh day; therefore the LORD blessed the sabbath day and made it holy."
>
> EXODUS 20:8–11

I RECENTLY NOTICED THAT in the English Standard Version of the Bible, the commandment about the Sabbath/rest is the longest of the Ten Commandments. It's really interesting to me that God spent more time explaining when, how, and why his people should rest than he did talking about idolatry, murder, etc. But when I think about how popular the "hustle hard" mindset is in our culture and the church, I can see why God elaborated on this commandment and even set the original example for rest when he created for six days and rested on the seventh.

Between work, hobbies, friendships, romantic relationships, kids, chores, girls' nights, side hustles, ministry, doom scrolling, streaming, and more, we don't give our bodies, minds, and hearts many chances to be still and be filled (Psalm 23 and Matthew 11:28-30). And yet, some things we do to chill out (like binge-watching *The Office* or videos on TikTok) give us a reprieve from physical activity without giving us the spiritual enrichment we need. Take a little time today to do a refreshing screen-free activity like the examples below, and consider praying or listening to the Bible while you do it. You could even focus on some passages that can help you process your emotions. A few of my favorites are Psalm 13, Psalm 31:23-24, Psalm 34:4-8, Psalm 42:5-6, Isaiah 40:29-31, Romans 5:3-5, Philippians 4:6-8, and James 1:19-20. Feel free to do more than one activity or combine a couple (like having a nice cup of coffee while you listen to worship music) if that would be spiritually enriching for you.

| | | |
|---|---|---|
| Going for a walk, jog, or run | Reading or listening to a Christian book | Knitting or crocheting |
| Gardening | Writing poetry | Drawing or painting |
| Using an adult coloring book | Cooking | Having a cup of coffee or tea |
| Swimming | Weightlifting | Riding a bike |
| Hiking | Getting a massage | Stretching |
| Listening to music | Playing a musical instrument | Taking a bath |

# Final Thoughts

"Now Barnabas wanted to take with them John called Mark. But Paul thought best not to take with them one who had withdrawn from them in Pamphylia and had not gone with them to the work. And there arose a sharp disagreement, so that they separated from each other. Barnabas took Mark with him and sailed away to Cyprus, but Paul chose Silas and departed, having been commended by the brothers to the grace of the Lord."

Acts 15:37–40

"Luke alone is with me. Get Mark and bring him with you, for he is very useful to me for ministry."

2 Timothy 4:11

As I referenced on day 22, Paul and Barnabas had "a sharp disagreement" about whether John Mark should join them on a missionary journey, and that conflict led to the men continuing their journeys separately. In the book of 2 Timothy, which Paul wrote when he was nearing his eventual execution, Paul specifically asked for John Mark—the same man he rejected as a partner in ministry many years before.

While we can see shining signs of reconciliation between those two men, we have no idea what transpired between the events of Acts 15 and the day Paul wrote that letter to Timothy. Did they run into each other at some point in their travels and have a serious discussion about John Mark's past abandonment at Pamphylia? Did John Mark send Paul a long letter filled with words of regret? Did Paul extend an olive branch and try to patch things up by apologizing for any wrong done on his end? And what happened to Barnabas? After he and John Mark returned to his native land of Cyprus, did he and Paul remain at odds, or did they also reconcile?

The fact that three men who we see as heroes in the faith had such a rocky season (or more) in their friendships can be a bit shocking, but it can also give us hope. If you're a Christian like they were, you have the same Holy Spirit in you who empowered them to do inspiring things, and the Spirit no doubt had a huge hand in the reconciliation between Paul and John Mark. It also means that the Spirit can work in *your* broken friendship and bring about reconciliation. He can also give you the power to glorify God while you process your former friendship and love your ex-BFF from afar, even if reconciliation never happens.

So, whatever happens between you and your former friend, remember these four things:

> God loves you perfectly and is perfectly in control of all your relationships.
>
> Your pain has a purpose that only he can reveal.
>
> His Holy Spirit will help you heal and grow faithfully.
>
> And even if this friendship is never rekindled, you are God's child, and you are *never* alone.

# About the Author

KRISTEN REED IS A native Texan and Black female author best known for writing *The Heart of a Harlot* and the Bible study *A Look At Luke*. She is a graduate of the University of Texas at Dallas, and her Christian faith heavily influences her writing and is the driving force in her life. She and her husband Noah reside in the Dallas area with their sons, Judah and Asa.

Official Website: kristenreedauthor.com
Instagram: @kristenreedtx

www.ingramcontent.com/pod-product-compliance
Lightning Source LLC
Chambersburg PA
CBHW071917160426
42813CB00098B/524